LOCAL RED BOOK

NORTHWICH WINSFORD

CONTENTS

Redbooks *showing the way*

very effort has been made to verify the accuracy of information in this book but the ublishers cannot accept responsibility for expense or loss caused by an error or omission.

formation that will be of assistance to the user of the maps will be welcomed.

he representation on these maps of a road, track or path is no evidence of the existence of a ght of way.

treet plans prepared and published by ESTATE PUBLICATIONS, Bridewell House, ENTERDEN, KENT. The Publishers acknowledge the co-operation of the local authorities of wns represented in this atlas.

Ordnance Survey® This product includes mapping data licensed from Ordnance Survey® with the permission of the Controller of Her Majesty's Stationery Office.

Legend

═══	Minor Road
▨▨▨	Pedestrianised / Restricted Access
═══	Track
⌐ ⌐	Built Up Area (Centre only)
- - - - -	Footpath
∼∼∼	Stream
∼∼∼	River
∼Lock∼	Canal
━━■━━	Railway / Station
●	Post Office
P P+▭▭▭	Car Park / Park & Ride
C	Public Convenience
+	Place of Worship
→	One-way Street
i	Tourist Information Centre
▲8	Adjoining Pages
▨▨	Area Depicting Enlarged Centre
▭	General Buildings (Centre only)
Woodland	Woodland
Recreation Ground	Recreation Ground
Cemetery	Cemetery

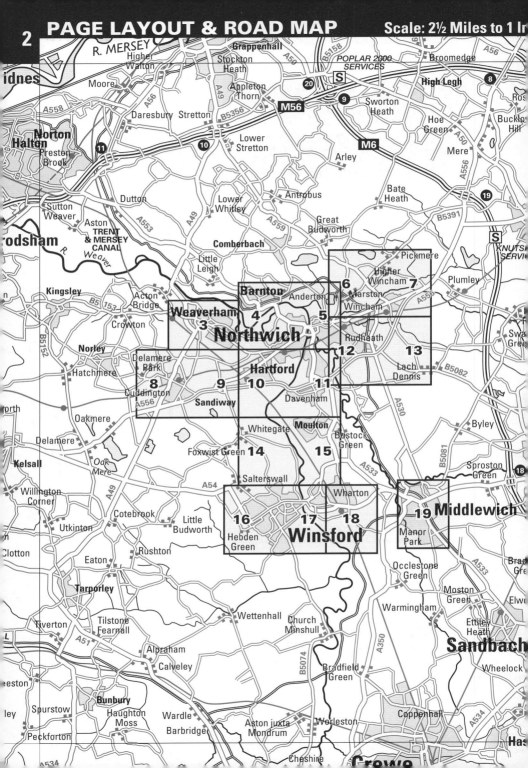

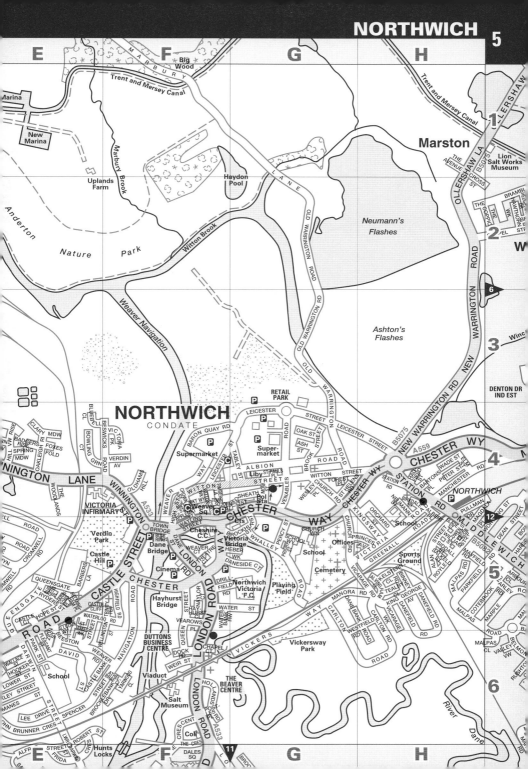

A   **B**   **C**   **D**

PAR

1

Pick Mere

Higher Marston

A559

M A R S T O N

Sewage Works

VALE RD
MERE RD
FERNLEA
MANOR AV
ROAD
HALL DR

HIELD

DARK LANE

Lane-ends Farm

Leigh Farm

Whalebone Farm

2

Marston Hall

OLLERSHAW LANE
B5075

L A N E

EARLES

M A R S T O N

School

3

OLLERSHAW LANE

Fields Farm

L A N E

CHURCH ST

B5381

Rosefarm Court

School Farm

Cemetery

Manor Farm

H A L L

GREEN

4

Trent and Mersey Canal

OLLERSHAW LA

Works

L A N E

Neumann's Flashes

Marston

THE AVENUE
CROSS ST
B5075
Lion Salt Works Museum

WINCHAM BUSINESS PARK

WINCHAM AV

Lodge Wood

Keepers Wood

5

◀ 5

OLLERSHAW LA

THE COPPICE
BRAMBLES
HEDGEROW
HAWTHORN
GORSE COVERT
BRACKEN WY
THE WK
CHAPEL STREET

WINCHAM

Works

OLD WARRINGTON ROAD

Wincham

WARRINGTON ROAD NEW

Witton Albion F.C.

CHESHIRE RING CANAL WALK

6

Ashton's Flashes

Wincham Brook

PRINCESS ST
BRICK ST
PRINCE ST
RENSHAW ST
HEWITT ST
BOUNDARY ST
STANLEY ST
GRO

M A N C H E S T E R

+

OLD WARR

KINGFISHER CT
HERON CT
DENTON DRI
AUSTIN ST
ANN ST
VAN
ORANGE ST

12

WORKS LA

DENTON DR IND EST

RO
A559

A   **B**   **C**   **D**

E **F** **G** **H**

1

Pickmere

2

Tanyard Farm

Providence Farm

Radio Telescope

Leonard's Wood

Smoker Wood

3

Higher Wincham

Home Farm

LINNARDS LANE

Smoker Brook

Hopley's Pipes

Pea's Wood

4

Winnington Wood

Holford Farm

Mill Wood

Lostock Gralam

A559 ROAD

CHESTER ROAD

A556 ROAD

5

Wincham Brook

Long Wood

School

Recreation Ground

LOSTOCK GRALAM

Home Farm

6

MANCHESTER ROAD

A556

E **F** **G** **H**

CUDDINGTON

Delamere Park

Cuddington

Bryn

The Riddings

The Home Farm

Works

Factory

Sewage Farm

Bryn Farm

Poplar Farm

Brook Farm

Town Moss

Gills Moss Wood

Manor Farm

Watermill Farm

Ravensclough

Cuddington Brook

Caravan Site

Oakmere Hall

Lobslack Wood

Oakmere Hall Farm

Lob Slack

Playing Field

Cartledge Moss

Library

School

CUDDINGTON

Sch

Roads and labels: BARRASTITCH LA, BAG LANE, CUDDINGTON LANE, MILL LANE, WARRINGTON ROAD, A49, SMITHY, MILLI, NORLEY ROAD, FOREST ROAD, CHESTER ROAD, A556, ROMAN ROAD, TARPORLEY RD, OVERDALE LANE, KENNEL, DALEFORDS, WEAVERHAM LANE, CHILTERN, LINKSAY, GREENFIELD, ROSSLYN LA, FARNDON CL, SANDOWN CRESCENT, EAST LANE, EAST CRES, BLAKE, IVY DR, KINGSLEY GATE, SCHOOL, SANDIWAY CL, MOORLANDS PK, MOORLANDS AV, MEADOW, GLEBE RD, MAYFIELD, MAYFIELD, CHERYL, BROOKSIDE, BRIDGE, TRICKETTS LA, VALLEY LA, MOSS, FOREST, CLOSE, WEST, NIXON RD, POPLAR, MOSS MERE, ROAD, CHERRY, GRANGE, MAPLE, BEECH, ACORN, OAK, LA SETT, ASH, MANOR, BOUNDARY ROAD, SANDINGTON DRI, MERE, WHARF, BURTON CL

Delamere Park area labels: THE SPINNEY, THE CHINES, ORCHARD DENE, DELAMERE PARK WAY WEST, THE WARREN, FAWNS, COPPERY WOOD, THE HOME FARM, WESTREES, PARK WAY WEST, THE BADGERS, THE ASPENS, THE DINGLE, LEAP, THE DELL, THE COPPICE, BURROWS, DENEHURST WAY, THE STILES, CUDDINGTON LANE, YEWLANDS, PADDOCK, FOXES HEY, LONG ACRE, WOODS LANE, THE DOWNS, CUSELDNBS, COPPLES, DELAMERE PARK WAY WEST, HOLLOW LA, OAK FIELDS, CEDARWOOD, THREENAYS, UPLANDS, WEST RAVENS, NORLEY ROAD

E   F   G   H

Gorstage Farm

Gorstage

Gorstage Green Farm

The Oaklands P.H.

LANE

GORSTAGE LANE

HODGE

ROAD

Brook Farm

Hartford Junction

Brownheath Farm

LANE

HODGE

Hodge Lane Farm

LITTLEDALES

LANE

HODGE

1

2

Rose Cottage Farm

sage Hall Farm

Moss Farm

Football Ground

10

HARTFORD BUSINESS PARK

ERHAM

LANE

Littledale's Gorse

CHESTER

LANE

SANDIWAY PK

ROAD

A559

HEYE PK

3

A556

Sandiway

Forest Hill Farm

LEY AV

SPRUCE AV

FIELDS

Club House

Vale Farm

4

ROAD

WAY

ROAD

10

HESTER

ROAD

POOL

LANE

Golf Course

5

COCKPIT

LANE

Petty Pool Wood

Petty Pool

6

E   F   G   H

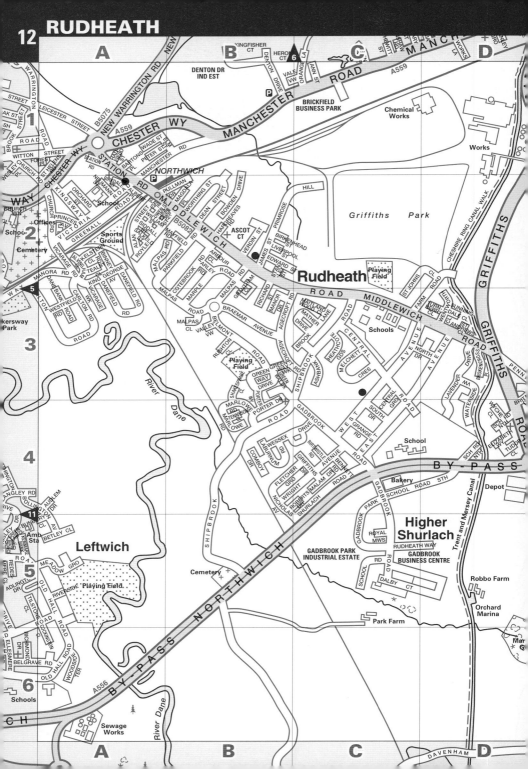

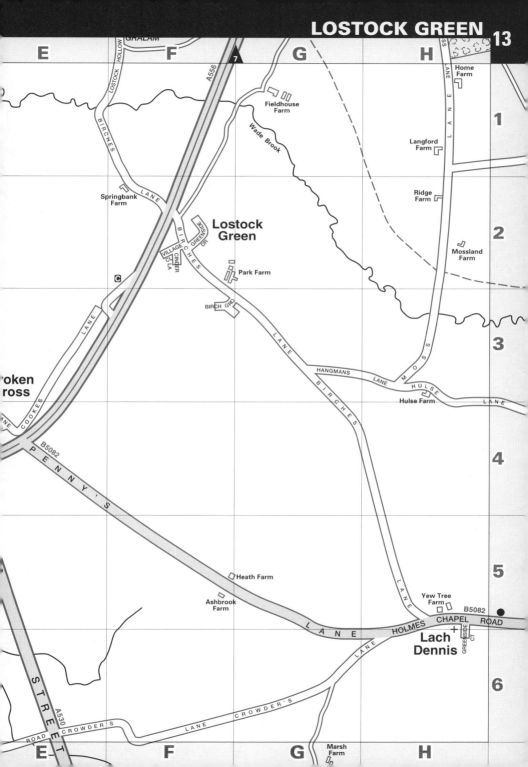

E F G H

GHALAM

LOSTOCK HOLLOW

BIRCHES

A556

Home
Farm

Fieldhouse
Farm

Wade Brook

Langford
Farm

1

LANE

Springbank
Farm

LANE

Lostock
Green

Ridge
Farm

BIRCHES

GREENSIDE DR

VILLAGE
GREEN
CL

CINDER
LA

Mossland
Farm

2

Park Farm

C

BIRCH GRO

LANE

3

COOKES

LANE

Broken
Cross

HANGMANS

LANE

MOSS

LANE

BIRCHES

HULSE

LANE

Hulse Farm

LANE

LANE

4

B5082

PENNY'S

5

Heath Farm

LANE

Yew Tree
Farm

B5082

Ashbrook
Farm

LANE

HOLMES

CHAPEL

ROAD

GREENSIDE CT

Lach
Dennis

6

STREET

A530

ROAD

CROWDER'S

LANE

CROWDER'S

LANE

Marsh
Farm

E F G H

Cookery Pool

Golf   Course

Valeroyal

New Pool

VALEROYAL COURTYARD

Valeroyal Park

Monks Well

ST MARY'S   DRIVE

ROYAL   DRIVE

VALE

SUTTON HILL

MILL

Eaton Wood

Whitegate

School

ABBEY CL

ABBEY FIELD

CINDER HILL

GRANGE LANE

GRANGE

Quesse Wood

MILL LANE COTTS

MILL   LANE

Newbri Wo

Parkside Farm

Foxwist Green

FOXWIST   GREEN

Foxwist Green Farm

GRANGE   LANE

LA

Pettypool Brook

Bradford Wood Farm

Meadow Ho Farm

Bogart Brook

WHITEGATE   WAY

Golf   Course

Knights Grange Sports Complex

Running Track

P.H.

GRANGE   LANE

Cat's Clough

Golf   Course

SANDRINGHAM CL

BALMORAL CL

MARLBOROUGH CL

SHENBROOK CL

SHEPHERDS

GLEN EAGLES CL

PRIORY CL

ALLANDALE

KNIGHTS

GRANGE LANE

TARN CL

ALDER DRIVE

BRAMBLE

HAWTHORN

WILLOW DRIVE

FOLD

ENNERDALE

BUTTERMERE

RYDAL CL

WEMWORTH GRO

Salterswall

WHITEGATE RD

CHEST RD

SUNNYW

ST MARYS

CAI

CUSTE

MUIRFIELD

BENB

E F G H

11

1

2

3

4

5

6

Peckmill

LONDON ROAD

A533

MEL
JACK LANE
FAIRHOLM AV
HAMLEIGH RD
POND
BANK

Bostockgrange
Farm

BRICK KILN LANE

**Bostock
Green**

Peckmill Brook

EATON
WEAVER GRANGE
VW
CHAPEL LA
THE HOLLIES
MA N
CHAPEL LA
BEECHFIELD LA

HARVEST CL
BARNSDALE DR
SUMMERFIELD DR

School

P

School

Hall

LAWRENCE CT
WHITLOW AV
REGENT ST
CHURCH
RD

Moultonbank
Farm

BARLOW
WILSON DR
WEAVER
WILSON DR
LODGE DR
HILLSIDE LANE
NIDDRIES VW
JAKESIDE VW

MEADOW LA
MEADOW LA
POPLAR
VERDIN CL
PARK LA
WHITLOW LA

ANTHONY DR

JACK LANE

Jack Lane
Farm

ROAD

SCHOOL LA

Caravan Site

Moulton

BRICK KILN LA

JACK LANE

Penmel's
Wood

Bostock
Farm

SMOKEHALL

LANE

WEAVER Navigation

BRADFORD ROAD

Meadow Bank
Farm

MEADOW GRO
HOOL
School
Playing Field

adowbank

Works

MEADOW BANK

ROAD

**INDUSTRIAL
ESTATE**

SMOKEHALL LANE

SMOKEHALL LANE

BOSTOCK LANE

Home
Farm

JACK LA

ROAD

A533

A5018

DEAKINS ROAD

THRUSH WAY

DEAKINS RD

HARTWELL GRO
COLLINGTREE
SHAWS WAY
UPTON
WHISTON CL
HOLCOT
CALDERTON
COLLINGTREE
EVERDON
CLINGTREE
HELMDON CL
DORTON
CL
CLAVER

**Wharton
Green**

Factory

Wharton
Bridge

ROAD
ONE

A5018

Factory

**PREMIER
PARK**

Factory

Works

VALLEY RD
WEAVER
A5018
COALPORT CL
THIRLMERE CL

WHARTON PARK ROAD

DOULTON RD
MAYFIELD DR
THE MAPLES
YNDALE
WHARTON GDNS

PARK AV

CROOK LANE

WHARTON RD

BRADBURY

DOWY RD

**WINSFORD
INDUSTRIAL
ESTATE**

ROAD ONE

ROAD
FOUR

**WHARTON
RETAIL
PARK**

Sewage Works

BRADFORD
LANE

Verdins Cut

**DONEFIELDS
INDUSTRIAL
ESTATE**

WHARTON HALL

NAT LANE
NAT LANE
NAT LANE

17

INGORE
SEVERN
WK

ESK ROAD
DEE WK
TAMAR WK
BRADF

B5355

E F G H

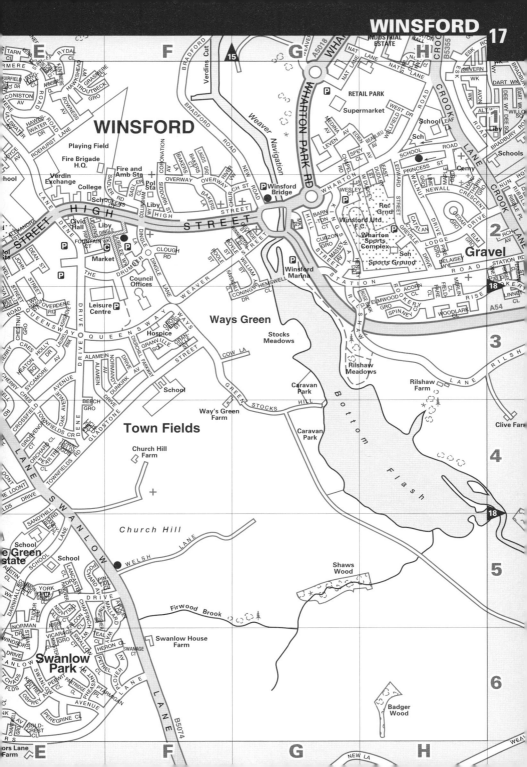

A
B
C
D
1
2
3
4
5
6
Wharton
WINSFORD INDUSTRIAL ESTATE
Works
PINEAPPLE PARK
Factory
Warehouse
Schools
Cemy
Liby
The Willowbeds
Stanthorne Hall Farm
Clive
Moss Rose Farm
Gravel
WINSFORD
Clive Hall Farm
Clive Farm
Double Wood
Mole Ho Farm
Pear Tree Farm
Clive Green
Park Fa
Shropshire Union Canal
Middlewich Branch
River Weaver
Wimboldsley Wood
Weaver Hall Farm
Top Flash
MIDDLEWICH
STATION ROAD
B5355
A54
CROOK LANE
RILSHAW LANE
CLIVE LANE
CLIVE BACK LA
CLIVE GREEN LANE
WEAVERHALL LANE
ROAD FOUR
ROAD FIVE
ROAD TWO
ROAD THREE
ION PATH
WALLACE CT
SEATON ST
HEWITT DR
BECKETT AV
NUN HOUSE DRIVE
NUN HO CL
DERWENT AV
RIBBLE PL
CLYDE CRES
CLYDE AVENUE
WHEELOCK DR
NUNSMERE CL
THAMES PL
MERSEY PL
DANE PL
AIRE PL
TRENT AV
TRENT CL
DOVE PL
BLYTHE PL
BOLLIN AV
BOLLIN CL
BRADBURY ROAD
DART WK
DEE WY
TAMAR WK
SEVERN
ESK
AVON WK
WILLOW SQ
DEE SQ
HAWTHORN GRO
CRESCENT
CEDAR DRIVE
BIRCH AV
GREENFIELDS
BEECHFIELDS
RISE
DIERDEN
LINNET CL
LINWOOD
ROOKERY
MERLIN
STATION RD
17

The Index includes some names for which there is insufficient space on the maps. These names are indicated by an * and are followed by the nearest adjoining thoroughfare.

A
Abbey Cl, Whitegate CW8 14 A2
Abbey Cl, Winsford CW7 17 E5
Abbey La CW8 10 B2
Abbey Way CW8 10 B3
Abbots Mere Cl CW8 8 C5
Abbots Way CW8 10 B3
Abbotts Way CW7 16 C1
Acorn Cl, Northwich CW8 8 C5
Acorn Cl, Winsford CW7 17 H3
Adlington Dr CW9 11 G2
Agecroft Rd CW9 12 B3
Ainsworth Rd CW8 3 E2
Aire PI CW7 18 A2
Aitchison Rd CW9 7 F6
Alamein Dr CW7 17 E3
Alamein Rd CW8 4 A1
Alan St CW9 5 H5
Albert PI CW9 5 H4
Albion Rd CW9 5 G4
Alder Rd CW8 3 D3
Alderley Rd CW8 5 E5
Alderton Gro CW7 15 F5
Aldford Way CW7 16 D1
Aldington Dr CW10 19 C6
Alexander Sq CW7 11 G1
Alexandra Rd CW10 19 C5
Alexandra St CW7 17 E2
Alfred St CW8 11 E1
Allcock Way CW8 5 E6
Allen Dr CW9 11 F5
Allgreave Cl CW10 19 B5
Almond Gro CW8 3 E4
Alt Walk CW7 17 H1
Alundale Rd CW8 14 C6
Alvanley Rise CW9 11 G1
Alvingham Cl CW9 5 H5
Ambleside Cl CW7 14 C6
Angus Gro CW10 19 C2
Ann St CW9 12 C1
Anthony Dr CW9 15 F2
Applefield CW8 4 D6
Applemarket St CW9 5 F5
Appleton St CW8 5 E4
Arbour Cl CW9 12 B2
Arkwright Cl CW7 16 C3
Arley Rd CW7 12 B2
Arnside Cl CW7 17 E1
Arthur St CW9 7 E6
Ascol Dr WA16 7 H4
Ascot Ct CW9 12 B2
Ash Gro, Middlewich CW10 19 C4
Ash Gro, Northwich CW8 3 E4
Ash Gro, Winsford CW7 17 E3
Ash Rd CW8 8 C5
Ash St CW9 5 G4
Ash Wood Cl CW8 4 B1
Ashbank CW9 12 C3
Ashfield St CW10 19 C3
Ashgate La CW9 7 E2
Ashley Dr CW8 10 A1
Ashley Grange CW9 7 E2
Ashmore Cl CW10 19 B6
Ashton Cl, Middlewich CW10 19 C6
Ashton Cl, Northwich CW9 11 E3
Ashwood Cres CW8 4 B2
Astbury Dr CW8 4 A1
Astle Cl CW10 19 B5
Aston Av CW7 16 C1
Aston Way CW10 19 D2
Athelbrae Cl CW8 5 F6
Audlem Dr CW9 11 G1
Austin Cl CW7 17 E5
Austin St CW9 6 C6
Avocet Dr CW7 17 F5
Avon Walk CW7 17 H1
Ayrshire Cl CW10 19 C2

B
Badgers Cl CW7 16 B2
Badgers Rise CW8 5 E4
Badgers Set CW8 8 A2
Bag La CW8 8 C1

Bakers Ct CW7 17 F1
Bakers La CW7 17 F2
Balmoral Av CW9 11 G2
Balmoral Cl CW7 14 C6
Bank Side CW8 3 C2
Barbers La CW8 5 E5
Barlow Dr CW7 16 B3
Barlow Rd CW9 15 F2
Barn Mdw CW8 5 E4
Barnbrook Cl CW7 16 C2
Barnside Way CW9 15 F1
Barnton Ct CW7 17 G2
Baron Quay Rd CW9 5 F4
Barrastitch La CW8 8 B1
Barrington Dr CW10 19 B5
Barrymore Rd CW8 3 E2
Bartons PI CW8 5 H4
Basford Way CW7 16 D1
Bateman Rd CW9 7 F6
Beach Gro CW8 10 C1
Beach Rd CW8 10 B1
Beagle Point CW7 16 B2
Beaulieu Av CW7 17 H1
Beaver Cl WA16 7 E1
Beckenham Gro CW7 16 C2
Beckett Av CW7 18 C3
Bedford Rise CW7 17 E5
Beech Cl CW8 8 C5
Beech Gro, Northwich CW8 3 E3
Beech Gro, Winsford CW7 17 E4
Beech Heyes Cl CW8 3 F3
Beech Heyes Dr CW8 3 F4
Beech La CW8 4 A2
Beech St CW10 19 B3
Beechfield CW9 15 E1
Beechfield Dr CW10 19 A1
Beechfield Gdns CW8 10 B1
Beechfields CW7 18 A2
Beechwood Av CW8 10 A1
Beechwood Dr CW9 7 E2
Beeston Cl CW10 19 C6
Beeston Dr CW10 16 D3
Beeston St CW8 5 E6
Belfry Cl CW7 16 C1
Belgrave Rd CW9 11 G3
Belmont Rd CW9 12 B3
Bembridge Ct CW10 19 B3
Bembridge Dr CW10 19 B3
Bennett Rd CW9 12 C4
Bentley Gro CW7 17 E5
Berkerley Rise CW7 16 C3
Berrystead CW8 10 C3
Beswicks Rd CW8 5 E4
Betley Cl CW9 11 G2
Bexton Av CW7 16 C1
Bickerton Way CW9 11 E3
Binney Rd CW9 5 H5
Birch Av CW7 18 A2
Birch Gro, Lostock Green CW9 13 F3
Birch Gro, Wincham CW9 7 E3
Birches La CW9 13 E1
Birkdale Ct CW9 5 H4
Birkdale CW9 12 A2
Birkenhead St CW9 12 B2
Birtwistle Rd CW9 12 C4
Bishopgates Dr CW9 11 E3
Blackcroft Av CW9 4 A3
Blackwell Cl CW10 19 C6
Blake La CW8 8 C5
Blakeden La CW7 16 A2
Blakelow Cl CW10 19 A4
Blakemere Dr CW9 11 E2
Blandford Dr CW9 11 E3
Blenheim Cl CW9 11 F3
Blenheim Gdns CW7 16 D4
Blossoms Heights CW8 4 D6
Bluebell Cl CW8 5 E4
Blythe PI CW7 18 A2
Boardmans PI CW9 11 F2
Bollin Av CW7 18 A1
Bollin Cl CW7 18 A1
Bollington Av CW9 11 G1
Bond St CW8 4 D4
Booth La CW10 19 C3
Booth Rd CW8 10 A3
Bosley Cl CW9 19 B5
Bostock Rd CW9 15 G5
Boundary La North CW8 8 C5
Boundary La South CW8 8 C5
Boundary St CW9 6 C6
Bowden Dr CW9 12 B2

Bowland Rise CW7 16 D4
Bowling Green Ct CW8 5 E4
Bowmere Dr CW7 17 E3
Bowness Av CW7 17 E1
Bracken Way, Barnton CW9 4 C2
Bracken Way, Wincham CW9 6 B5
Brackenfield Way CW7 16 B2
Bradburns La CW8 10 B1
Bradbury Rd CW7 15 E3
Braddon Cl CW9 11 F3
Bradford Rd CW8 15 E3
Bradley Cl CW10 19 A4
Braemar Av CW7 12 B3
Bramble Cl CW7 14 C6
Bramble Way CW10 19 D2
Bramhall Cl CW7 16 D2
Bramhalls Pk CW8 4 C2
Brecon Way CW7 16 D3
Brereton Rd CW8 10 B3
Briar La CW8 15 G2
Brick Kiln La CW10 15 G2
Brickfield Bsns Pk CW9 12 C1
Bridge Cl CW8 8 C3
Bridge La CW8 8 C3
Bridge St CW9 6 D6
Bridgemere Way CW9 11 E3
Bridgewater PI CW7 16 C2
Brindley Av CW7 16 D2
Brittania Dr CW9 12 D4
Broadway CW8 4 B2
Brockhurst St CW9 5 F5
Brockhurst Way CW9 11 G1
Brocklebank Dr CW8 5 G1
Brockwell Cl CW7 16 C3
Broken Cross PI CW9 12 D3
Brook La CW9 12 C3
Brook La, Northwich CW9 5 G4
Brook La, Wincham CW9 6 D6
Brooklands CW10 19 A2
Brooklands Dr CW9 11 G3
Brooks La CW10 19 C2
Brooks La Ind Est CW10 19 C3
Brookside, Cuddington CW8 8 C3
Brookside, Weaverham CW9 3 C2
Broomfield Cl CW7 16 B3
Broomsfield La CW8 4 A1
Browning Way CW7 16 B4
Broxton Av CW10 19 C6
Brunner Mond Winnington Works CW8 4 D3
Brynlow Av CW10 19 A4
Brynlow Dr CW10 19 A4
Buckfast Way CW10 19 A2
Buckingham Dr, Northwich CW9 11 E2
Buckingham Dr, Winsford CW7 16 D4
Buckley Cl CW10 19 A4
Bull Ring CW9 5 F5
Bunbury Cl, Middlewich CW10 19 B6
Bunbury Cl, Northwich CW9 11 G1
Burgess PI CW8 5 E5
Burland Gro CW7 16 C2
Burnside Way CW8 4 D4
Burrows Hill CW8 4 C6
Burwardsley Way CW9 11 E3
Butley Cl CW10 19 B5
Buttercup Way WA16 7 E1
Buttermere Rd CW7 17 E1
Byley Cl CW10 19 D1
Byley Way CW7 16 D2
Byron Cl CW10 19 C6

C
Caerleon Cl CW7 16 B3
Caernarvon Av CW7 16 D4
Caister Way CW7 16 D1
Calderbank Way CW10 19 C2
Caldicott Cl CW7 16 D4
Caldy Way CW7 16 D2
Calveley Cl CW9 11 E2
Calveley Way CW7 16 C2
Cambrian Way CW7 16 D3
Cambridge Av CW7 16 C2
Campbell Cl CW9 11 F3
Canal Side CW8 4 B3
Canal Ter CW10 19 C3
Canton CW8 5 G4

Capesthorne Cl CW9 11 F3
Carden Av CW7 16 C2
Carisbrook Dr CW7 16 D4
Carlisle Cl CW7 16 C2
Carlton Rd CW9 5 G5
Carmarthen Cl CW7 16 D4
Carnoustie CW7 16 C1
Cartledge Cl CW8 8 D4
Cartmel Cl CW7 17 E1
Carver Cl CW7 15 G5
Castle Bank CW8 5 E6
Castle Cliff CW8 5 E5
Castle Cl CW8 5 E5
Castle St CW8 5 E5
Castlemead Walk CW9 11 E3
Catalan Cl CW7 17 H2
Cavendish Cl CW7 16 C3
Cedar Cl, Middlewich CW10 19 D6
Cedar Cl, Northwich CW8 7 F5
Cedar Dr CW8 4 B1
Cedar Gro CW7 17 H2
Cedar Rd CW8 3 D3
Cedarwood CW8 8 A2
Central Dr CW8 4 A2
Central Gro CW8 12 C4
Central Rd CW9 12 C3
Centurion Way CW10 19 B1
Chadwick Cl CW10 19 C5
Chadwick Rd CW10 19 B5
Chaffinch Way CW7 17 E5
Chantry Av CW8 10 B3
Chapel Cl CW9 5 F6
Chapel La CW9 15 E1
Chapel Rd CW7 17 G1
Chapel St, Weaverham CW8 3 D2
Chapel St, Wincham CW9 6 B5
Chapel St*, Beeston St CW9 5 E6
Charles Av CW9 11 H5
Chartley Gro CW10 19 C1
Chartwell Gro CW7 17 E6
Chatsworth Cl CW9 11 G2
Chepstow Cl CW7 16 D4
Cherry Cres CW7 17 E3
Cherry La, Cuddington CW8 8 C4
Cherry La, Weaverham CW9 3 E3
Cherry Tree Av CW8 4 B1
Cherrywood Cres CW8 4 B1
Cheryl Ct CW8 8 C3
Chester La CW7 16 A1
Chester Rd, Cuddington CW8 8 B6
Chester Rd, Middlewich CW10 19 A4
Chester Rd, Northwich CW8 4 B3
Chester Rd, Winsford CW7 16 A1
Chester Way CW9 5 F5
Chesterfield Cl CW7 16 B2
Chesterton Cl CW10 19 D6
Chestnut Cl, Middlewich CW10 19 A1
Chestnut Cl, Northwich CW8 8 C5
Chestnut Gro CW7 17 E3
Cheviot Cl CW7 16 D4
Chilham Cl CW7 16 D4
Chillingham Cl CW10 19 C1
Chiltern Cl CW8 8 D5
Chiltern Way CW7 16 C4
Chipstead Cl CW8 10 A2
Chirk PI CW7 16 B2
Christleton Av CW7 11 G3
Church Cl CW8 3 D2
Church La CW8 3 D2
Church Rd, Barnton CW8 4 B3
Church Rd, Northwich CW9 5 G4
Church Rise CW8 8 D5
Church St, Davenham CW9 11 G4
Church St, Moulton CW9 15 F1
Church St, Weaverham CW8 3 D2
Church St, Wincham CW9 6 D4
Church St, Winsford CW7 17 G2
Church Walk CW9 5 G5

Churchfields, Churchfields CW8
Churchfields, Sandiway CW8
Churchill Parkway CW7
Churton Cl CW9
Cinder La CW8
Civic Way CW10
Clare PI CW7
Claremont Cl CW9
Clary Mdw CW8
Cledford Cres CW10
Cledford La CW10
Cleveland Way CW9
Clifford PI CW7
Clifton Dr CW9
Clitheroe Rd CW8
Clive Back La CW7
Clive La CW7
Clivegreen La CW7
Clough La CW8
Clough Rd CW7
Clover Dale CW8
Clover Dr, Knutsford WA16
Clover Dr, Winsford CW7
Clyde Cres CW7
Coalport Dr CW7
Cockington Cl CW8
Cockpit La CW8
Collingham Way CW7
Collingtree Av CW7
Comboy Dr CW9
Commonwealth Cl CW7
Coningsby Dr CW7
Coniston Av CW7
Conway Av CW7
Cookes La CW9
Copper Wood CW8
Coppice Dr CW10
Corfe Way CW7
Coriander Cl CW7
Coronation Av CW7
Coronation Gro CW8
Coronation Rd CW10
Coronet Av CW9
Cotebrook Rd CW9
Cotswold Cl CW8
Cotswold Way CW7
Court La CW8
Covert Cl CW7
Cow La CW7
Cranmere Cl CW8
Cresanne Cl CW10
Crocus St CW8
Crofters Lea CW8
Croftwood Cl CW7
Cromwell Rd CW8
Crook La CW7
Cross La CW10
Cross St, Barnton CW8
Cross St, Marston CW9
Crossbridles Cl CW8
Crossfield Av CW7
Crowders La CW9
Crown St CW9
Croxton La CW10
Croxton Way CW8
Crum Hill CW9
Cuddington La CW8
Curlew Cl CW7
Curzon Gro CW7
Cusel Nest CW8
Cypress Mws CW8

D
Daisy Bank La CW8
Daisy Cl WA16
Dalby Ct CW7
Dale Ct CW10
Dalefords La CW8
Dales Sq CW9
Dalmahoy Cl CW7
Dalton Way CW10
Dane Bank Rd CW9
Dane PI CW7
Dane St, Middlewich CW10
Dane St, Northwich CW9
Danefield Rd CW9
Daneside Ct CW9
Dark La CW9
Darlington St CW7
Darnhall School La CW7

Walk CW7 18 A1
win St CW8 5 E6
enham Ct CW9 11 G4
enham Way CW10 19 C6
d St CW8 5 E6
ins Rd CW7 15 G5
n St,
  dlewich CW10 19 B2
n St,
  thwich CW9 12 B2
sford CW7 17 E2
Sq CW7 18 A1
Way CW7 18 A1
isey Way CW7 17 H2
mere Cl CW8 4 B2
mere Pk Way East
  8
mere Pk Way West
  8
mere Rise CW7 16 D2
mere Cl CW7 16 C1
igh Cres CW10 19 B4
igh Dr CW7 16 D2
e Dr CW7 17 E2
hurst Park Way
  8 A2
on Cl CW7 16 D2
on Dr CW9 6 B6
on Dr Ind Est
  9 12 B1
vent Av CW7 18 A2
on Cl CW10 19 C2
er Way CW10 19 C1
den St CW7 18 A2
dens Ter CW10 19 B3
le La CW7 17 F2
le Walk CW7 17 E2
le Way CW8 8 B2
ma Dr CW10 19 B1
ells Rd CW9 11 F2
Rd CW9 5 F6
efields Ind Est
  7 15 G6
glas Cl CW8 10 C2
ton Cl CW7 15 F6
e Pl CW7 18 A1
r Dr CW7 16 C4
ield Rd CW9 5 F5
don Cl CW9 11 F3
es Way CW9 11 E2
am Rd CW9 11 E2
kirk Av CW7 17 F3
ore Cl CW10 19 G3
ster Cl CW9 11 G3
am Dr CW7 16 D4
ns Bsns Centre
  9 5 F6
Ter CW9 4 D4
esfield CW8 10 C3
swick Rd CW10 19 B6
s La CW9 6 C2
Way CW9 11 F3
Av CW9 12 C4
Dudley St CW7 17 H1
La CW8 8 D4
Rd CW10 19 A3
Cres CW9 11 E5
Dr CW10 19 A4
La CW9 11 E5
Pl CW8 10 A3
Vw CW9 15 E1
Cl CW7 15 G5
sbury Way CW9 11 E4
Av CW7 17 G1
ard St CW9 12 B2
ton Av CW8 10 B3
eth Way CW9 12 D4
mere Rd CW9 11 G2
ham Way CW9 11 E4
Rd CW7 17 H2
Rd,
  dlewich CW10 19 C3
Rd,
  thwich CW8 3 E3
St CW9 5 H4
idge Way CW8 4 D4
wood Gro CW7 17 H3
wood Rd CW9 4 B1
nett St CW8 3 E2
rdale Cl CW7 14 D6
Way CW10 17 H1
Rd CW7 17 H1
ale Cl CW7 14 C6
ers La CW8 3 E3
don Cl CW7 15 F5
n Cl CW9 11 E1
View Cl CW8 4 A2
cre Dr CW10 19 C6
eld Rd CW9 11 G2
eld Walk CW10 19 C5
olm Rd CW9 15 G1
ak Cl CW7 16 B3

Falcon Cl,
  Middlewich CW10 19 C6
Falcon Cl,
  Winsford CW7 17 E5
Fallon Ct CW10 19 B4
Fallowfield Cl CW7 16 B2
Faraday Rd CW8 4 D3
Farley Cl CW8 19 A3
Farm Cl CW8 3 D2
Farm Rd,
  Rudheath CW9 12 C3
Farm Rd,
  Weaverham CW8 3 D2
Farndon Cl CW8 8 D4
Farriers Way CW7 16 B2
Faulkner Dr CW10 19 B5
Fawns Leap CW8 8 B2
Fearnleigh CW8 4 C6
Fern Way CW8 3 D2
Fernbank Cl CW7 18 A2
Fernlea Rd CW9 6 A2
Fernleigh Cl,
  Middlewich CW10 19 D6
Fernleigh Cl,
  Winsford CW7 16 B2
Field Cl CW8 4 C6
Fieldfare Cl CW7 17 H2
Fieldway CW8 3 C2
Finneys La CW10 19 A2
Finsbury Walk CW7 16 C2
Fir Gro CW8 3 E3
Fir La CW8 8 C4
Fir Tree Cl CW8 4 B1
Firdale Rd CW8 4 C6
Firthfields CW8 11 F5
Firthfields Cl CW9 11 F4
Firtree Cl CW7 18 A2
Fitton St CW9 7 E6
Flavian Cl CW10 19 B2
Flea La CW10 19 B3
Fletcher Gro CW9 12 B4
Flower St CW8 5 E6
Ford Ct CW7 8 C4
Forest Cl CW8 8 C4
Forest Pl CW8 5 G4
Forest Rd,
  Northwich CW8 8 B6
Forest Rd,
  Winsford CW7 16 C3
Forest St CW8 3 C3
Forster Av CW8 3 E3
Fossa Cl CW10 19 B1
Fountain Ct,
  Northwich CW9 11 F5
Fountain Cl,
  Winsford CW7 17 E2
Fountain La CW9 11 F5
Fountains Cl CW10 19 A2
Foxendale Cl CW8 4 D6
Foxes Fold CW8 5 E4
Foxes Hey CW8 8 A2
Foxfield La CW7 16 B2
Frida Cres CW8 11 E1
Fryer Rd CW7 7 F5
Fullerton Rd CW8 10 A2
Fulton Gro CW9 11 F4
Furness Cl CW7 16 D3

Gadbrook Bsns Centre
  CW9 12 C5
Gadbrook Pk Ind Est
  CW9 12 C5
Gadbrook Rd CW9 12 C4
Galloway Cl CW9 19 C1
Garfit St CW10 19 C2
Gawsworth Cl CW9 11 G2
Geneva Rd CW7 17 E2
George St,
  Northwich CW8 4 B2
George St,
  Winsford CW7 17 G2
George VI Av CW10 19 C5
George VI Cl CW10 19 C5
Gerrard Dr CW8 3 E2
Gibbon Dr CW9 7 F5
Gladstone St,
  Northwich CW8 5 E6
Gladstone St,
  Winsford CW7 17 E4
Glastonbury Dr CW10 19 A3
Gleave Rd CW8 3 E2
Glebe Green Dr CW7 16 D5
Glebe Rd CW8 8 D3
Gleneagles Dr CW7 16 D1
Gold Crest Cl CW7 17 E6
Goodwood Cl CW8 4 B2
Goodwood Rise
  CW10 19 A2
Gordale Cl CW8 4 D4
Gorse Covert CW8 6 B5
Gorsley Cl CW10 19 B6
Gorstage La CW8 3 C3
Gough Cl CW7 19 C3
Gowy Walk CW7 15 G6

Graingers Rd CW9 11 F2
Grampain Way CW7 16 C4
Grange Av CW8 4 B2
Grange La,
  Northwich CW8 3 B4
Grange La,
  Whitegate CW8 14 A2
Grange La,
  Winsford CW7 16 D1
Grange Lea CW10 19 A2
Grange Rd,
  Cuddington CW8 8 C5
Grange Rd,
  Rudheath CW9 12 C4
Grangebrook Dr CW9 14 C6
Grantham Cl CW9 12 B3
Granville Rd CW9 11 G2
Granville Sq CW7 17 F3
Granville St CW7 17 F3
Grasmere Cl CW7 17 E1
Green Av,
  Barnton CW8 4 A2
Green Av,
  Davenham CW9 11 F4
Green La,
  Davenham CW9 11 F4
Green La,
  Wincham CW9 6 D4
Green Pk CW8 3 E4
Green Walk CW8 8 D3
Greenall Rd CW9 5 H5
Greenbank La CW8 10 D1
Greendale Dr CW10 19 A4
Greenfield Way CW8 8 D3
Greenfields CW7 18 A2
Greenlaw CW7 11 G2
Greenside Cl CW8 13 H6
Greenside Dr CW9 13 F2
Greenway Dr CW9 12 B3
Greenway Walk CW9 12 B3
Greenwood Cl CW8 3 D2
Greville Dr CW7 17 H2
Griffiths Dr CW9 12 C4
Griffiths Rd CW9 12 D2
Grosvenor Av CW8 10 B3
Grosvenor Cl CW7 17 F3
Grosvenor St CW7 17 F3
Grove Av CW8 7 E5
Grove Cl CW7 16 C3
Grovemount CW9 11 F5
Guernsey Cl CW10 19 C2

Hadfield St CW9 5 H4
Hadrian Way,
  Middlewich CW10 19 B1
Hadrian Way,
  Northwich CW8 9 E5
Hall Dr CW9 6 A2
Hall La CW9 6 D4
Hall View Cl CW8 3 B4
Hambleton Way CW7 16 C4
Hampstead Ct CW7 16 C3
Handley Hill CW7 16 D3
Hangmans La CW9 13 G3
Hankelow Cl CW10 19 B5
Hannahs Walk CW10 19 A3
Hanover Dr CW7 17 E5
Harewood Cl,
  Northwich CW9 11 F2
Harewood Cl,
  Winsford CW7 16 B2
Hargreaves Rd CW9 12 B2
Harris Rd CW9 7 F6
Harrisons Pl CW8 5 E5
Hartford Bsns Park
  CW8 10 A3
Hartford Rd CW9 11 E4
Harthill Cl CW9 11 E2
Hartwell Gro CW7 15 F5
Harvest Cl CW9 15 F1
Hatherton Cl CW9 11 F3
Hatton La CW8 10 D1
Haweswater Dr CW7 17 E1
Hawkshead Way CW7 17 E1
Hawthorn Cl CW7 14 D6
Hawthorn Gro CW7 17 H2
Hawthorn Rd CW9 3 D3
Hawthorn Walk CW9 6 B5
Hawthorne Gro CW8 4 A1
Hayes Dr CW8 4 C2
Hayhurst Av CW10 19 A4
Hayhurst Cl CW9 5 F5
Hazel Dr,
  Northwich CW8 3 E3
Hazel Dr,
  Winsford CW9 17 E3
Hazelmere Cl CW8 10 C2
Hazelwood Cl CW8 4 B1
Headworth Cl CW9 11 F2
Heath Rd CW8 3 E2
Heathcote Gdns CW9 12 C3
Heaton Cl CW8 19 B5
Heaton Sq CW7 17 E3
Heber Walk CW9 5 F5
Hedgerow Dr CW9 6 B5

Hefferston Grange Dr
  CW8 3 B3
Hefferston Rise CW8 3 B4
Helmdon Cl CW7 15 G5
Helmingham Pl CW7 5 E5
Hemming St CW8 4 D3
Hemswell Cl CW7 17 G2
Henbury Cl CW10 19 B5
Henley Dr CW7 17 G2
Herbert St CW9 7 E6
Hereford Way CW10 19 C2
Heron Cl CW7 17 E6
Heron Ct CW9 6 B6
Hesketh Dr CW9 7 F5
Hewitt Dr CW7 18 C3
Hewitt Gro CW9 7 E3
Hewitt St CW8 6 C6
Heyes Pk CW8 10 A3
Heyeswood La CW8 10 A3
Heysoms Av CW8 4 D6
Heysoms Cl CW8 4 D6
Hickson St CW8 4 B2
Hield La CW9 6 B1
High St,
  Northwich CW9 5 F5
High St,
  Weaverham CW8 3 C2
High St,
  Winsford CW7 16 D2
High Town CW10 19 B2
Highbank Cl CW8 4 B2
Highbank Rd CW8 4 D6
Highfield Av CW9 7 F5
Highfield Rd CW8 5 F5
Hill St CW7 17 G2
Hill Top CW7 17 G2
Hill Top Av CW9 16 D2
Hill Top Rd CW8 3 A1
Hill View Rise CW8 5 E4
Hillside CW8 4 D6
Hillside La CW9 15 E2
Hilton Cl CW10 19 B4
Hinchley Cl CW8 10 A2
Hindley Cres CW8 4 B2
Hodge La CW9 9 F1
Holcot Ct CW9 15 G5
Holford Av CW9 7 F5
Hollands Rd CW9 5 F6
Hollow Oak La CW8 8 A3
Holly Ct CW10 19 A2
Holly Dr CW7 17 E3
Holly Rd CW8 3 D3
Holly Walk CW8 4 C6
Hollybank Cl CW8 4 D3
Holmes Chapel Rd,
  Middlewich CW10 19 C2
Holmes Chapel Rd,
  Northwich CW9 13 H6
Homewood Cres
  CW8 10 B2
Hooker St CW8 5 E6
Hope St CW8 5 E5
Hough La CW9 4 C1
Houghton Cl CW9 11 F3
Hubert Dr CW10 19 B4
Hulse La CW9 13 H3
Hunters Fld CW8 3 D2
Hunters Hill CW8 3 D2
Hunters Rise CW7 16 D2
Hunts La CW9 9 E4
Hurdsfield Cl CW10 19 B4
Hutchins Cl CW10 19 D5
Huxley St CW8 5 E6

Inglewood Av CW10 19 C6
Ion Path CW7 18 B2
Ivy Dr CW8 8 D5

Jack La,
  Davenham CW9 11 G6
Jack La,
  Moulton CW9,10 15 G1
James St CW9 12 B2
Jersey Way CW10 19 C2
John Brunner Cres
  CW8 5 E6
John Fryer Av CW9 7 E3
John St,
  Northwich CW9 5 F4
John St,
  Winsford CW7 17 E2
Joyce Av CW7 17 E1
Jubilee Way CW7 17 F2

Keats La CW9 7 F3
Keepers La CW8 3 F4
Kelsborough Cl CW9 11 E4
Kelstern Cl CW9 5 H5
Kendrick Cl CW8 3 D2
Kenmare Bank CW9 11 G2
Kensington Cl CW7 17 E4
Kensington Way CW9 11 E4
Kentmere Av CW7 17 E1
Kents Ash CW7 17 E4
Kerridge Cl CW10 19 A4

Kestrel Cl,
  Middlewich CW10 19 C6
Kestrel Cl,
  Winsford CW7 17 E6
Kestrel Rd CW8 4 D6
Keswick Cl CW7 14 D6
Kinderton St CW9 19 C2
King Edward Cl CW9 11 F2
King Edward St CW10 19 B3
King George Av CW9 5 H5
King St, Hartford CW8 10 C2
King St,
  Middlewich CW10 19 B2
King St,
  Rudheath CW9 13 E5
King St Ind Est
  CW10 19 B1
Kingfisher Cl CW8 6 B6
Kingfisher Dr CW7 17 E5
Kingfisher Gro CW9 6 D3
Kings Cres CW9 19 B1
Kings Gate CW8 8 D5
Kingsley Cl CW9 10 C2
Kingsley Dr CW9 11 G1
Kingsley Walk CW7 16 C1
Kingsmead CW9 11 F3
Kingsmead Sq Retail Pk
  CW9 11 E2
Kingsway,
  Northwich CW9 5 G4
Kingsway,
  Winsford CW7 17 G2
Kingswood Cres
  CW10 19 D6
Kintore Cl CW9 15 G6
Kitfield Av CW10 19 B4
Knights Mdw CW7 14 C6
Knightsbridge Av CW9 11 F4

Laburnum Gro CW8 3 E3
Laburnum Rd,
  Davenham CW9 11 F4
Laburnum Rd,
  Rudheath CW9 12 B4
Ladies Walk CW10 19 B4
Lagos Gro CW7 17 F1
Lakehouse Cl CW8 3 D2
Lakeside Vw CW9 15 F2
Lambert Way CW8 10 A3
Lambourne Gro CW10 19 B2
Lancaster Cl CW7 17 E5
Landswood Pk CW8 10 C2
Langdale Cl CW7 17 E1
Langford Rd CW9 7 E5
Langley Cl CW9 11 G1
Lapwing Cl CW7 17 E6
Larch Cl CW8 3 E4
Larch Tree Cl CW8 4 C1
Latham St CW7 17 E2
Launceston Cl CW7 16 D4
Laurel Bank CW7 17 E3
Laurel Cl,
  Middlewich CW10 19 A1
Laurel Cl,
  Northwich CW8 4 B1
Lavender Dr CW9 12 D3
Lavister Cl CW9 11 F3
Lawnsdale CW8 8 A2
Lawrence Av CW9 15 E1
Lawrence Av East
  CW10 19 B2
Lawrence Av West
  CW10 19 B2
Laxton Way CW10 19 B2
Lea Wood Cl CW8 10 A1
Leadsmithy St CW10 19 B2
Leaf Gro CW7 16 C2
Leaf La CW7 17 H1
Leafy Way CW8 3 E4
Ledward St CW7 17 H1
Lee Dr CW8 5 E6
Leicester St CW9 5 F4
Leigh Way CW8 3 D2
Leighs Brow CW8 4 A2
Leslie Rd CW8 16 B4
Leven Av CW7 17 G1
Lewin St CW10 19 B3
Leyland Walk CW7 17 E5
Lichfield Ct CW7 17 E4
Lichfield St CW10 19 C2
Lift La CW9 4 D2
Lilac Dr CW8 4 D6
Lime Av,
  Northwich CW9 11 F1
Lime Av,
  Weaverham CW8 3 D3
Lime Cl CW10 19 A1
Lime Ct CW9 11 F1
Lime Gro CW7 17 H2
Limewood Cres CW8 4 B1
Limewood Gro CW8 4 C1
Lindisfarne Cl CW10 19 A2
Lindsay Walk CW8 8 D3
Linnards Cl CW9 7 E2
Linnet Cl CW7 18 A3

Street	Ref
Linton Cl CW7	15 G6
Linwood CW7	18 A3
Lister Cl CW10	19 C6
Littledales La CW8	9 G1
Littler Grange Ct CW7	16 B2
Littler La CW7	16 A3
Littleton Cl CW9	11 F3
Liverpool St CW9	12 B2
Livingstone Way CW10	19 C6
Llandovery Cl CW7	16 D4
Lodge Dr, Moulton CW9	15 F2
Lodge Dr, Winsford CW7	17 H2
Lodge La, Hartford CW8	10 C3
Lodge La, Lostock Gralam CW9	7 F5
Lodge La, Middlewich CW10	19 D2
London Rd, Davenham CW9	11 F3
London Rd, Northwich CW9	5 F5
Long Acre, Cuddington CW8	8 A2
Long Acre, Weaverham CW8	3 C2
Long La CW10	19 B3
Long La South CW10	19 B5
Long Mdw CW8	3 C2
Long Moss Cl CW10	19 B4
Long Mynd Rise CW7	16 D3
Longcross Ct*, Civic Way CW10	19 B3
Longhorn Cl CW10	19 C1
Longwood CW10	19 B4
Lostock Hollow CW9	13 F1
Lower Darwin St CW8	5 E6
Lower Haigh St CW7	17 E3
Lower St CW10	19 B2
Ludlow Cl CW7	16 D4
Lulworth Cl CW7	16 D4
Lydyett La CW8	4 B2
Lymcote Dr CW8	10 A2
Lyndale Ct CW7	15 G6
Lytham Dr CW7	16 D1
Magdala Pl CW9	12 B3
Maidenhills CW10	19 C3
Maidwell Cl CW7	15 G5
Main Rd CW9	15 E1
Maitland Wood Cl CW9	12 C3
Malam Dr CW9	12 C4
Mallard Way CW7	17 F5
Malmesbury Cl CW10	19 A3
Malpas Cl CW7	12 B3
Malpas Rd CW9	12 A3
Malvern Way CW7	16 C3
Manchester Rd CW9	11 G1
Manley Cl CW7	11 G1
Manor Av CW9	6 A2
Manor Cres CW10	19 B5
Manor Dr, Barnton CW8	4 B3
Manor Dr, Rudheath CW9	12 B3
Manor Flds CW10	19 B4
Manor Gro CW8	10 C1
Manor La CW10	19 B3
Manor Rd CW8	8 C5
Manor Sq CW7	16 C3
Manor St CW8	4 D6
Maple Ct CW7	15 G6
Maple Gro, Barnton CW8	4 B1
Maple Gro, Northwich CW8	4 C6
Maple Gro, Winsford CW7	17 H2
Marbury Rd CW9	4 D1
Marford Cl CW9	11 E2
Market Pl CW7	17 G2
Market St CW9	5 F4
Market Way CW9	5 F4
Marlborough Av CW7	14 C6
Marlowe Rd CW7	12 B4
Marple Rd CW8	12 B3
Marshall La CW8	10 D1
Marshalls Ct CW8	10 C2
Marston La CW9	6 A1
Massey Av, Northwich CW8	10 B3
Massey Av, Winsford CW7	17 G2
Mather Cl CW10	19 B3
Mather Dr CW9	12 C3
Mayfair Dr CW9	11 F3
Mayfield Dr, Northwich CW8	8 D3
Mayfield Dr, Winsford CW7	15 G6
Mayfield Gro CW8	8 D3
Mayfield Rd CW9	12 B2
Meadow Cl, Northwich CW8	8 D3
Meadow Cl, Winsford CW7	14 C6
Meadow Dr CW8	4 A1
Meadow Gate CW9	7 E3
Meadow Gro, Northwich CW9	11 G2
Meadow Gro, Winsford CW9	15 E4
Meadow Home Pk CW9	15 E3
Meadow La CW9	15 F2
Meadow Rd CW8	3 F3
Meadow Rise CW7	16 B2
Meadow St CW9	5 G4
Meadow Vw CW10	19 A1
Meadowside CW8	4 D6
Medina Av CW7	17 G1
Melchett Cres CW9	12 C3
Mendip Cl CW7	16 D3
Mere Bank CW9	11 G6
Mere Cl WA16	7 F1
Mere La, Pickmere WA16	7 E2
Mere La, Sandiway CW8	8 D4
Mere Rd CW9	6 A2
Merehaven Cl WA16	7 E1
Mereworth Dr CW9	11 F2
Merlin Cl CW7	17 H2
Mersey Pl CW7	18 A2
Mervyn Rd CW8	3 E2
Middlehurst Av CW8	3 F3
Middlewich Rd, Northwich CW9	12 A2
Middlewich Rd, Winsford CW7	18 B2
Midpoint 18 Ind Est CW10	19 D2
Mill La, Cuddington CW8	8 C2
Mill La, Middlewich CW10	19 C2
Mill La, Newtonia CW10	19 A3
Mill La, Whitegate CW8	14 A2
Mill La Cotts CW8	14 B2
Millbrook Ct CW7	16 B2
Milley La WA16	7 G1
Millgate CW8	8 C3
Millington La CW8	8 D1
Milner Rd CW8	10 D1
Milton Cl, Middlewich CW10	19 C6
Milton Cl, Northwich CW9	12 A2
Minster Cl CW7	17 E6
Monarch Dr CW9	11 E2
Mond St CW8	4 B2
Monks Way CW8	4 B2
Montgomery Way CW7	16 C4
Moor Park Way CW9	11 F3
Moorlands Av CW8	8 D3
Moorlands Pk CW8	8 D3
Moors La CW7	17 E6
Moreton St CW8	4 D4
Moreville Cl CW9	11 E3
Mornant Av CW8	10 A3
Morris Dr CW8	3 E2
Morris Pk CW8	10 C3
Moss Bank CW7	16 D2
Moss Dr CW10	19 C5
Moss La, Cuddington CW8	8 C4
Moss La, Lostock Green CW9	13 H3
Moss La, Northwich CW8	4 D5
Moss Rd CW8	4 D4
Moss St CW8	3 D2
Moss Ter CW8	4 D4
Mottram Cl CW9	19 A5
Mouldsworth Cl CW9	11 E3
Moulton Cl CW9	11 E3
Mount Pleasant Dr CW7	16 C3
Mount Pleasant Rd CW9	11 F4
Muirfield Cl CW9	11 G2
Muirfield Dr CW7	17 E1
Mulberry Rise CW8	4 C6
Nantwich Rd CW10	19 A4
Nat La CW7	17 G1
Navigation Rd CW8	5 F6
Naylor Ct CW9	5 F5
Needham Dr CW8	10 B3
Neumann St CW9	5 H4
New King St CW10	19 B1
New Rd, Northwich CW9	4 D2
New Rd, Winsford CW7	17 G1
New Warrington Rd CW9	5 H4
Newall Cres CW7	17 H2
Newbury Av CW7	16 C3
Newton Bank CW10	19 A2
Newton Hall Mews CW10	19 B3
Newton Heath CW10	19 A2
Nicholas Av CW9	12 B4
Nicholas Rd CW8	3 E2
Niddries La CW9	15 F2
Nightingale Cl CW10	19 C6
Nightingale Ct CW7	17 E5
Nixon Dr CW9	11 G6
Nixon Rd CW8	8 C4
Norbury Dr CW10	19 A4
Norbury St CW9	5 H5
Norley Rd CW8	8 A3
Norman Dr CW7	17 E6
Normandy Av CW7	16 C3
Nor Dr CW9	12 C3
Northway CW8	4 D4
Northwich By-Pass CW9	11 F3
Northwich Rd CW8	3 D2
Northwood Av CW10	19 D6
Nun House Cl CW7	18 A2
Nun House Dr CW7	18 A2
Nunsmere Cl CW7	18 A2
Nursery Rd CW8	4 B2
Oak Av CW7	17 E4
Oak Dr CW9	19 C5
Oak House La CW7	17 E4
Oak La CW8	8 C5
Oak Mdw CW8	3 F4
Oak St CW9	5 G4
Oakleigh Rise CW8	5 E4
Oakmere Rd CW7	16 A1
Oaktree Cl CW8	4 C1
Oakwood La CW8	4 A2
Oddfellows Pass*, Pinfold La CW10	19 A2
Old Gate Cl CW10	19 A4
Old Hall Rd CW9	11 G2
Old Road CW9	4 D4
Old School Cl CW8	4 B2
Old Vicagage La CW8	10 C2
Old Warrington Rd CW9	5 G2
Oldhams Hill CW8	5 F4
Ollershaw La CW9	6 B2
Orange La CW9	12 C1
Orchard Cl, Barnton CW8	4 B2
Orchard Cl, Middlewich CW10	19 C4
Orchard Cl, Weaverham CW8	3 E2
Orchard Cl, Wincham CW9	7 E2
Orchard Cl, Winsford CW7	17 E4
Orchard Ct CW8	3 D2
Orchard Dene CW8	8 A2
Orchard Gdns CW8	3 C2
Orchard St CW9	5 H4
Orton Cl CW7	15 G5
Osprey Av CW7	17 G6
Osprey Cl CW7	19 C6
Otters Bank CW7	16 C2
Over Hall Dr CW7	17 E4
Overdale La CW8	8 A6
Overdene Rd CW7	17 E3
Overton Cl CW10	19 A3
Overway CW7	17 F2
Owen St CW9	5 H5
Owley Wood Rd CW8	3 E2
Paddock Vw CW10	19 B1
Paddock Walk CW8	8 A2
Palmer Cl CW7	11 F2
Park Av, Northwich CW8	3 D2
Park Av, Winsford CW7	15 G6
Park Cres CW8	8 C3
Park La, Hartford CW8	10 B3
Park La, Northwich CW9	15 F2
Park La, Pickmere WA16	7 E1
Park Rd, Middlewich CW10	19 B3
Park Rd, Northwich CW8	4 D4
Park St CW9	5 H4
Parker Av CW8	10 A1
Parkfield Rd CW9	12 B2
Parkside CW9	11 H2
Parliament St CW8	5 E6
Partridge Cl CW7	17 E6
Partridge Way CW7	7 E3
Paulden Rd CW9	7 F6
Peacock Av CW7	16 D5
Pear Tree Cl CW7	17 E4
Pear Tree Dr CW9	7 E2
Peckforton Way*, Beeston St CW9	5 E6
Peewit Cl CW7	17 E6
Pembroke Way CW7	16 C3
Pennine Way CW7	16 C3
Pennys La CW7	12 D3
Penrhyn Rd CW8	5 E5
Pentland Cl CW7	16 C3
Pepper St CW10	19 B2
Percy St CW9	5 G5
Peregrine Cl CW7	17 E6
Peter St CW9	5 H4
Petrel Cl CW7	17 E6
Pheasant Dr CW9	6 D3
Pheasant Way CW7	17 E6
Pickmere La CW7	7 E2
Picton La CW7	11 F3
Picton Dr CW7	16 C1
Pine Gro CW7	17 H2
Pineapple Pk CW7	18 A1
Pinetree Cl, Northwich CW8	4 B1
Pinetree Cl, Winsford CW7	18 A2
Pinewood Rd CW7	16 C2
Pinfold La CW10	19 A2
Pinfold Way CW8	3 D2
Pintail Cl CW7	17 E5
Pipers Ash CW7	16 C2
Pippin Cl CW9	19 B4
Plantagenet Cl CW7	17 E5
Pleasant St CW8	5 E6
Plover Av CW7	17 E6
Plumbs Fold CW8	4 A2
Pochard Av CW7	17 E6
Pochin Way CW10	19 D2
Pond Cl CW9	15 G1
Pool La CW8	9 E5
Poole St CW7	17 F2
Poplar Av CW9	15 F1
Poplar Cl, Northwich CW8	8 C4
Poplar Cl, Winsford CW7	16 C3
Poplar Dr CW10	19 C3
Poplar Rd CW8	3 D3
Porter Dr CW9	12 B4
Porter Way CW9	12 B3
Portman Pl CW7	16 C2
Post Office Pl*, Albion Rd CW8	5 G4
Postles Pl CW9	5 F6
Prestbury Cl CW9	11 F3
Prestwick Cl CW7	17 E1
Primrose Hill, Cuddington CW8	8 C3
Primrose Hill, Rudheath CW9	12 B2
Princes Av CW9	5 G5
Princes Pk CW8	4 B2
Princess Cres CW9	19 C5
Princess St, Northwich CW9	6 D6
Princess St, Winsford CW7	17 H1
Priory Av CW9	11 F2
Priory Cl CW7	14 C6
Priory St CW9	5 G5
Priory Way CW8	10 B3
Pritchard Dr CW9	11 E5
Prospect Dr CW9	11 E4
Prosperity Way CW10	19 C2
Ptarmigan Pl CW7	17 E6
Pulford Cl CW9	11 E3
Pulford Rd CW7	16 D4
Pullman Dr CW9	12 A2
Quantways CW8	10 C3
Quantock Cl CW9	16 C4
Queen St, Middlewich CW10	19 B3
Queen St, Northwich CW9	5 F6
Queens Cl CW7	17 F2
Queens Dr CW10	19 C5
Queens Par CW7	17 E2
Queensgate CW8	5 E5
Queensway CW7	17 E3
Redshaw Cl CW10	
Redstone Dr CW7	
Redwwood Cl CW8	
Regal Cl CW9	
Regency Ct CW7	
Regency Way CW9	
Regent St CW9	
Regents Way CW7	
Registry Cl CW9	
Renshaw Rd CW9	
Ribble Av CW9	
Ribble Pl CW7	
Richard St CW9	
Richmond Dr CW7	
Riddings La CW8	
Rilshaw La CW7	
River Vw CW7	
Riverside CW9	
Riverside Pk CW8	
Road Beta CW10	
Road Five CW7	
Road Four CW7	
Road One CW7	
Road Three CW7	
Road Two CW7	
Robert St CW8	
Roberts Dr CW9	
Roberts Rd CW9	
Roehurst La CW7	
Rolt Cres CW10	
Romanes St CW8	
Rookery Gdns CW9	
Rookery Rise CW7	
Rose Bank Cl CW7	
Rosebank Walk CW8	
Rosetree Mdw CW7	
Rosewood Dr CW7	
Rosselt Cl CW9	
Rosslyn La CW7	
Rowan Cl, Middlewich CW10	
Rowan Cl, Winsford CW7	
Rowan Rd CW8	
Rowan Rise CW8	
Rowton Cl CW9	
Royal Gdns CW9	
Royal Mws CW9	
Roylance Dr CW10	
Royle St, Northwich CW9	
Royle St, Winsford CW7	
Royles Pl CW8	
Rudheath Way CW9	
Runcorn Rd CW8	
Rushton Cl CW9	
Rushton Dr CW10	
Russell Rd CW7	
Russet Cl CW10	
Russet Rd CW8	
Rutland Dr, Middlewich CW10	
Rutland Dr, Northwich CW9	
Rydal Cl CW7	
Ryders St CW8	
Ryecroft Cl CW10	
Sadler Cl CW7	
Sadler Rd CW7	
St Andrews Cl CW9	
St Annes Av CW10	
St Annes Rd CW10	
St Bedes Av CW8	
St Catherines Dr CW8	
St Chads Flds CW7	
St Georges Rd CW7	
St Georges Way CW9	
St Helens Rd CW7	
St James Ter CW7	
St James Walk CW7	
St Johns Av CW9	
St Johns Cl CW9	
St Johns Dr CW7	
St Johns Gdns CW7	
St Johns Way CW7	
St Marys Av CW8	
St Marys Dr CW8	
St Michaels Way CW10	
St Pauls Pl CW9	
St Vincent Dr CW8	
Salkeld St CW9	
Samian Cl CW7	
Sandfield La CW8	
Sandington Dr CW8	
Sandiway CW7	
Sandiway Pk CW8	
Sandown Cl CW10	
Sandown Cres CW8	
Sandringham Cl, Northwich CW9	
Sandringham Cl, Winsford CW7	

La CW8 3 C1
hill Pl CW7 17 E5
hill Rd CW7 17 E5
mere Ct CW7 16 D2
all Cl CW9 11 E3
Crossway CW7 16 D2
s La CW8 4 D6
l Dr CW8 4 A2
l La,
ck Gralam CW9 7 F6
l La,
wich CW9 15 F1
l La,
iway CW8 8 D5
l Rd,
lowbank CW7 15 E4
l Rd,
wich CW9 12 C5
l Rd,
ford CW7 17 H1
l Rd North CW9 12 D4
l Rd South CW9 12 C4
l Walk CW10 19 B3
l Way CW9 5 G5
ank CW10 19 C2
ave Cl CW9 11 F1
n St CW7 18 C2
n St CW10 19 B2
n Walk CW7 17 H1
brook La CW8 3 C2
speare Cl CW9 12 B3
ngton Way CW9 11 F3
s La CW7 15 F2
n St CW9 5 G4
y Av CW9 7 E2
y Cl CW10 19 C6
erds Fold Dr 14 C6
n Cl CW10 19 D6
rook Rd,
nham CW9 11 G4
rook Rd,
eath CW9 12 B5
s Green Dr CW9 7 E3
horn Cl CW10 19 C1
shire Cl CW10 19 B3
ch Rd CW9 12 C5
l St CW9 5 H5
gton Av CW9 11 G2
rn St CW7 17 F2
dale CW8 4 D6
onds Cl CW9 11 E4
swood Cl CW10 19 A4
St CW9 5 H5
wood Cl CW10 19 B4
s La CW8 3 D2
y La,
ck Gralam CW9 7 F6
y La,
iway CW8 8 D1
ehall La CW7 15 G4
don St CW8 4 A2
donia Way CW7 16 D4
Rd CW8 4 D3
Hill CW9 4 C2
Dr CW9 12 C4
wark Pl CW7 16 C3
way CW10 19 B2
eighn Cl CW9 12 D4
er St,
ton CW8 4 B2
er St,
wich CW8 5 E6
Cl CW7 17 G1
La WA16 7 F1
ey Cl CW7 17 H3
Mdw CW8 5 E4
bank Cres CW7 17 E3
field Cres CW8 4 A1
fields CW8 8 A3
ston Way CW9 11 E3
e Av CW8 9 E4
el Cl CW8 4 D6
Ct CW8 3 C2
d Way CW10 19 B3
ford Dr CW9 11 G2
rd Cl CW9 11 F2
y Cl CW8 10 A3
y Gro CW9 6 D6
y St CW9 12 B2
y Cl CW9 11 E3
n Rd,
n Bridge CW8 3 A1
n Rd,
ck Gralam CW9 7 E6
n Rd,
wich CW9 5 H4

Station Rd,
Winsford CW7 17 G2
Staveley Dr CW7 17 E1
Steele Rd CW10 19 C6
Stephenson Walk CW7 16 C3
Sterling Cl,
Northwich CW9 11 F1
Sterling Cl,
Winsford CW7 15 G6
Stocks Hill CW7 17 G4
Stone Heyes La CW8 4 A1
Stones Manor La CW8 10 C2
Stretton Walk CW9 11 F3
Stuart Cl CW7 17 E6
Stubbs La CW9 7 F5
Styal Cl CW9 11 F3
Summerfield Dr CW9 15 F1
Sunningdale Cl,
Northwich CW9 12 D3
Sunningdale Cl,
Winsford CW7 16 C1
Sutton Cl CW9 7 E2
Sutton Fld CW8 14 A2
Sutton La CW10 19 B6
Swallow Ct CW7 17 E6
Swanage Ct CW7 17 F6
Swanlow Av CW7 17 E6
Swanlow Dr CW7 17 E6
Swanlow La CW7 16 D3
Swanscoe Cl CW10 19 A4
Sweet Briar Cl CW8 4 B1
Sycamore Av CW7 17 E3
Sycamore Cres CW8 4 B1
Sycamore Dr CW10 19 C6
Sydney St CW8 4 D6
Sylvan Cl CW8 4 C6

Tabley St CW9 5 G4
Tall Trees Cl CW8 4 C6
Tamar Walk CW7 15 G6
Tarn Cl CW7 14 D6
Tarporley Rd CW8 8 B6
Tarvin Cl CW10 19 C6
Tatton Cl,
Northwich CW9 11 F3
Tatton Cl,
Winsford CW7 16 D2
Teal Cl CW7 17 E6
Tealby Cl CW9 5 H5
Tefler Ct CW10 19 D6
Telford Way CW10 19 D2
Tennyson Cl CW9 12 B4
Tewkesbury Cl CW10 19 A3
Thames Pl CW7 18 A2
The Aspens CW8 8 B2
The Avenue CW9 6 A5
The Beaver Centre
CW9 5 F6
The Brambles CW9 6 B5
The Burrows CW8 8 A2
The Chines CW8 8 A2
The Close CW8 10 D1
The Cobbles CW8 8 A2
The Coppice,
Cuddington CW8 8 A2
The Coppice,
Wincham CW9 6 B5
The Corners CW8 3 E4
The Courtyard CW8 3 B3
The Crescent,
Hartford CW8 10 A2
The Crescent,
Middlewich CW10 19 A2
The Crescent,
Northwich CW9 11 F1
The Crescent,
Weaverham CW8 3 E2
The Dell CW8 8 A2
The Dingle CW8 4 B1
The Downs CW8 8 A2
The Drumber CW7 17 E2
The Fairways CW7 16 C1
The Grange CW8 10 B2
The Green,
Middlewich CW10 19 C6
The Green,
Northwich CW8 10 B2
The Hawthorns CW8 4 C6
The Hollies CW9 15 E1
The Loont CW7 17 E4
The Maples CW7 15 G6
The Mews CW8 4 B2
The Moorings CW10 19 B2
The Nursery CW8 10 C1
The Orchards WA16 7 E1
The Paddock CW8 10 C3
The Pavilions CW9 11 E5

The Spinney CW8 8 A2
The Stiles CW8 8 B2
The Warren CW8 8 A2
The Weavers CW10 19 B2
The Willows CW9 7 E2
The Windings CW10 19 A1
The Woodlands,
Northwich CW8 5 E4
The Woodlands,
Wincham CW9 7 E2
Theatre Ct CW9 5 F5
Thilmere Cl CW7 15 F6
Thistle Cl WA16 7 E1
Thorn Cl CW8 10 C2
Thornton Cl CW7 15 G6
Thornycroft CW7 16 C2
Threeways CW8 8 A3
Thrush Way CW7 15 F5
Tiffield Ct CW7 15 G5
Tilstone Cl CW9 11 G2
Timber La CW9 5 F4
Tower La CW8 3 C2
Town Bri CW8 5 F5
Town Sq CW9 5 F4
Townfield Ct CW8 4 B1
Townfield La CW8 4 A1
Townfields Cres CW7 17 E4
Townfields Dr CW7 17 E5
Townfields Gdns CW7 17 E4
Townfields Rd CW7 17 E4
Townsend Rd CW9 7 E5
Trafalgar Cl CW9 11 E4
Trent Av CW7 18 A2
Trent Cl CW7 18 A2
Trickett La CW8 8 D4
Trinity Ter CW8 5 F5
Troutbeck Gro CW7 17 E1
Tudor Cl,
Northwich CW9 12 D4
Tudor Cl,
Winsford CW7 17 E5
Tunnel Rd CW8 4 B3
Turnberry Cl,
Northwich CW9 12 D3
Turnberry Cl,
Winsford CW7 17 E1
Tytherington Cl CW10 19 B5

Ullswater Av CW7 17 E1
Uplands CW8 8 A3
Upper Haigh St CW7 17 E3
Upton Cl CW7 15 F5

Vale Rd, Hartford CW8 10 C3
Vale Rd, Marston CW9 6 A2
Vale Royal Dr CW8 14 A2
Vale Vw CW9 12 B1
Valeroyal Courtyard
CW8 14 B1
Valley La CW8 8 C4
Valley Rd CW8 3 C2
Valley Vw CW9 12 B3
Vauxhall Way CW7 16 D5
Vearows Pl CW9 5 F5
Venables Rd CW9 5 G4
Venables Way CW10 19 D6
Ventnor Cl CW10 19 B3
Verdin Av CW8 5 F4
Verdin Cl,
Moulton CW9 15 F2
Verdin Cl,
Winsford CW7 16 D1
Verdin St CW9 12 B2
Vicarage Gro CW7 17 E6
Vicarage Rd CW9 5 G5
Vicarage Walk CW9 5 H5
Vickers Way CW9 5 G6
Victoria Pk CW8 5 F4
Victoria Rd CW9 5 H5
Victoria Sq CW7 16 C3
Victoria St CW9 6 C6
Village Cl CW9 13 F2

Wade Cres CW8 4 A1
Wade St CW9 5 H4
Wades La CW7 14 C6
Walker Dr CW10 19 B4
Wallace Ct CW7 18 C2
Wallace St CW8 5 E6
Wallerscote Rd CW8 3 D3
Walmer Pl CW7 16 D5
Walnut Dr CW7 17 H2
Walnut La CW8 10 A2
Walnut Rd CW8 3 D3
Wardle Mws CW10 19 C4
Warmingham La
CW10 19 C5

Warren Av CW9 7 E5
Warren Cl CW10 19 A4
Warren La CW8 10 B3
Warrington Rd CW8 8 C3
Warwick Pl CW7 16 D5
Waste La CW8 8 B4
Water Edge Mews
CW10 19 B4
Water St CW9 5 F5
Waterbank Row CW9 5 F5
Waterloo Rd CW8 5 E5
Waters Edge CW9 4 D1
Waterside Vw CW9 12 D4
Waterside Way CW10 19 A1
Watling St CW9 5 F5
Wavertree Dr CW10 19 A4
Ways Grn CW7 17 F3
Waystead Cl CW9 11 F3
Weaver Ct CW9 5 F5
Weaver Grange CW9 15 E1
Weaver Rd,
Moulton CW9 15 F2
Weaver Rd,
Northwich CW8 5 E6
Weaver Sq CW9 5 F4
Weaver St CW7 17 F3
Weaver Valley Rd CW7 15 F6
Weaver Vw CW8 3 D2
Weaver Way CW9 5 F4
Weaverham By-Pass
CW8 3 B1
Weaverham Rd CW8 8 D5
Weaverton Cl CW9 11 E3
Webbs La CW10 19 B1
Weir St CW9 5 F6
Welbeck Cl CW10 19 A3
Well La CW8 3 C1
Well St CW7 17 E2
Wellfield CW7 17 H1
Wellfield Cl WA16 7 F1
Wellington St CW8 5 E6
Welsh La CW7 17 F5
Wentworth Cl CW9 12 D3
Wentworth Gro CW7 14 B6
Wesley Ct CW7 17 G2
Wesley Pl CW9 5 G4
Wessex Dr CW9 12 B4
West Av,
Middlewich CW10 19 B2
West Av,
Northwich CW9 12 C4
West Dr CW7 17 H1
West Dudley St CW7 17 H2
West La CW8 8 C4
West Rd CW8 3 C2
West St CW10 19 B3
West Wood Ct CW7 17 E3
Westbury Cl CW10 19 B4
Westfield Cl CW7 17 E6
Westfield Gro CW8 4 A1
Westfield Rd CW9 5 G6
Westgate Cl CW7 16 C2
Westlands Rd CW10 19 A3
Westminster Cl CW10 19 A2
Westminster Gro CW7 16 C3
Weston Cl CW10 19 B4
Westrees CW8 8 A2
Whalley Rd CW9 5 G5
Wharburton Cl CW8 8 C5
Wharton Gdns CW7 15 G6
Wharton Hall CW7 15 G6
Wharton Park Rd CW7 17 G1
Wharton Rd CW7 17 G2
Wharton Retail Pk
CW7 15 F6
Wheatfield Cl CW8 4 A2
Wheelock Dr CW7 18 A2
Wheelock St CW10 19 B2
Whirley Cl CW10 19 B5
Whiston Cl CW7 15 G5
Whitbys La CW7 16 C2
White Horse Alley
CW10 19 B3
White Park Cl CW10 19 C1
Whitegate Cl CW10 19 B5
Whitegate Way CW7 14 A5
Whitehall Cl CW8 4 A1
Whitehall Dr CW8 10 C2
Whitehart Gdns CW8 10 A3
Whitelodge Mews CW8 8 D3
Whitemore Rd CW10 19 B5
Whitley Av CW8 4 B2
Whitley Cl CW10 19 A4
Whitley Dr CW8 10 B3
Whitlow La CW9 15 F1
Whittington Gdns
CW9 11 F5

Wilbraham Rd CW8 3 E2
William St,
Northwich CW9 5 H5
William St,
Winsford CW7 17 G2
Willow Cl CW7 14 D6
Willow Ct CW10 19 B2
Willow Grn CW8 3 D3
Willow Gro CW8 4 B1
Willow Sq CW7 18 A1
Wilsbury Grange CW8 10 A2
Wilson Cres CW9 7 F5
Wilson Dr CW9 15 F2
Wilton Cl CW9 11 E3
Wincham Av CW9 6 C5
Wincham Bsns Park
CW9 6 C5
Wincham La CW9 6 B5
Windermere Rd CW7 17 E1
Windsor Cl CW8 8 C3
Windsor Dr CW7 17 E6
Wingfield Pl CW7 16 D5
Winnington Av CW8 4 C6
Winnington La CW8 4 C2
Winnington St,
Northwich CW8 5 F4
Winnington St,
Winsford CW7 17 G2
Winsford Ind Est
CW7 18 C1
Withens Cl CW8 3 D3
Withens La CW8 3 D3
Withington Cl CW9 11 G1
Witton St CW9 5 F4
Witton Walk CW9 5 F4
Woburn Cl CW9 11 E2
Wolvesey Pl CW7 16 D5
Wood La CW8 3 F3
Woodcott Av CW7 16 C2
Woodend Cl CW10 19 B5
Woodford La CW7 16 C3
Woodford La West
CW7 16 B4
Woodford Pk Ind Est
CW7 16 B4
Woodham Cl CW8 10 D2
Woodlands Gro CW8 4 A1
Woodlands Rd CW8 10 C2
Woodlark Cl CW7 17 H3
Woodlea Ct CW8 4 D6
Woodpecker Dr CW9 11 F3
Woodside Ter CW9 11 H3
Woodstock Dr CW10 19 D6
Woodward St CW8 3 D2
Works La CW9 6 D6
Worleston Cl CW10 19 B5
Worthing St CW9 12 B2
Wright Av CW9 12 B4
Wych House La CW10 19 C3
Wyche Cl CW9 12 D4
Wyncroft Ct CW8 3 D2
Wyndham Cl CW9 11 F2

Yarwood Cl CW8 5 F6
Yew Tree Cl CW10 19 A1
Yew Tree Dr CW8 4 B1
Yewlands CW8 8 A1
York Dr CW7 17 E5

Zion St CW8 5 E6

Edition 591-03 07-03

For an up-to-date publication list and latest prices visit our web site at

www.estate-publications.co.uk

Use the search facility to find the village, town or city you require.

Local Red Books (selection of)

Ashford & Tenterden
Barnstaple & Bideford
Basildon & Billericay
Basingstoke & Alton
Bath & Bradford-upon-Avon
Bedford
Brentwood
Bromley (London Borough)
Burton-upon-Trent & Swadlincote
Cambridge
Chelmsford, Braintree & Maldon
Chester
Chesterfield
Chichester & Bognor Regis
Colchester & Clacton
Crewe
Eastbourne, Bexhill, Seaford & Newhaven
Exeter & Exmouth
Fareham & Gosport
Folkestone, Dover, Deal & Romney Marsh
Gloucester & Cheltenham
Gravesend & Dartford
Great Yarmouth & Lowestoft
Hereford
Ipswich & Felixstowe
Kidderminster

Kingston-upon-Hull
Lancaster & Morecambe
Lincoln
Macclesfield & Wilmslow
Maidstone
Medway & Gillingham
Newport & Chepstow
Northampton
Norwich
Oxford & Abingdon
Peterborough
Plymouth, Saltash & Torpoint
Reading & Henley-on-Thames
Redditch & Bromsgrove
Rugby
Salisbury, Amesbury & Wilton
Sevenoaks
Southend-on-Sea
Stafford
Swindon
Telford
Tunbridge Wells & Tonbridge
Warwick & Royal Leamington Spa
Weston-super-Mare & Clevedon
Winchester
York

Super Red Books

Birmingham (Colour)
Bournemouth
Brighton
Bristol
Cardiff
Coventry
Derby
Edinburgh
Glasgow
Leicester
Nottingham
Portsmouth
Southampton (Colour)
Stoke-on-Trent
Swansea

County Red Books

Bedfordshire
Berkshire
Buckinghamshire
Cambridgeshire
Cheshire
Cornwall
Derbyshire
Devon
Dorset
Essex
Gloucestershire
Hampshire
Herefordshire
Kent
Leicestershire & Rutland

Lincolnshire
Norfolk
Northamptonshire
Nottinghamshire
Oxfordshire
Shropshire
Somerset
Staffordshire
Suffolk
Surrey
Sussex (East)
Sussex (West)
Warwickshire
Wiltshire
Worcestershire

Estate Publications, Bridewell House, Tenterden, Kent, TN30 6EP
Tel: 01580 764225 Fax: 01580 763720